Pip, Jim and Dan are in the den.
'Kids! Come and get some drinks and crisps!' yells Frank, Jim and Dan's dad.

Jim tilts his drink and spills it on Dan. Dan is cross. Dan jumps up and stamps on Jim's crisps. Jim is cross.

Jim is mad and spits at Dan. Dan is mad and yells at Jim, 'I'll tell Dad you spat and he will not let you in the den!'

Pip was upset. 'Stop it, Dan. Stop it, Jim!' said Pip. But Dan and Jim did not stop. 'Dan is a wimp,' said Jim. 'Jim is a brat,' said Dan.

Slam! Pip stomps off. 'Pip, come back,' said Jim.
'Pip, don't sulk,' said Dan. But Pip just ran off.

Pip trots up the hill. Dan runs up as well. 'Pip, stop!' But Pip has fled. She runs past the pond. She is still cross.

It's wet and Dan slips on a clump of grass. He twists his leg and falls flat. The damp smell of moss hits him. It stinks.

Dan's leg is stiff. 'Oh no. I can't stand up. But I must not panic.' He grunts and props his leg up on a tree trunk.

Dan yells, 'Pip! Pip! Help!' Pip stops. She runs back and spots Dan in the tall grass. Pip helps Dan lift his leg and stand up.

Dan drags his leg. He pants. He huffs and puffs. He limps to the pond. 'My leg is stiff, Pip,' Dan sobs. He sniffs. 'I can't go on. I must just rest a sec.'

'You just rest,' said Pip. 'I can run and get help.'
She sped off.

'Frank, Dan fell. You must come and help him!'
'It's not one of Dan's pranks, is it?' said Frank.
'No. He can't stand up. He's next to the pond.'

Jim sobs.

Pip says, 'Don't get upset, Jim. Frank went to get Dan. Trust me, Frank will help him. It will end well.'

'Dad!' yells Dan.

'Dan, sit still. Let's get you up. I can lift you.' Dan's dad swept him up and set off.

'Prop the leg up or it will swell,' Frank said. 'The skin on the leg is red, but it's not cut and hasn't bled. It was just a bad twist. Just rest it.'

Dan says, 'Pip, you ran and got help. You are a pal.'
Jim clasps Pip's hand. 'Pip, you are the best pal!'
'And you? Are you pals?' Pip asks. Jim grins. Dan grins. 'Best pals.'